Joseph T. Walker
School

Donated by
Chuck Rutherfoord

1984

John Young

Space Shuttle Commander

by Paul Westman

DILLON PRESS, INC. MINNEAPOLIS, MINNESOTA

Library of Congress Cataloging in Publication Data

Westman, Paul
  John Young, space shuttle commander.

  (Taking part)
  SUMMARY: A biography of the astronaut who made the fifth space flight
of his twenty-year career as commander of the space shuttle Columbia.
  1. Young, John (John Watts), 1930 -   —Juvenile literature.
  2. Astronauts—United States—Biography—Juvenile literature.
  [1. Young, John (John Watts), 1930 -   . 2. Astronauts] I. Title.
  TL789.85.Y67W47   629.4'092'4 [B] [92]   81-15264

  ISBN 0-87518-223-2   AACR2

© 1981 by Dillon Press, Inc. All rights reserved

Dillon Press, Inc., 500 South Third Street
Minneapolis, Minnesota 55415

Printed in the United States of America
  5· 6 7 8 9 10 11 12 13 92 91 90 89 88 87 86 85 84

JOHN YOUNG

As the commander of the Space Shuttle *Columbia,* John Young showed why he is known as one of America's greatest astronauts. The 50-year-old Young guided *Columbia* to a picture-perfect landing on a sunbaked runway in California's Mojave Desert. *Columbia*'s flight capped a 20-year career as an astronaut that included a record-breaking five spaceflights.

John Young grew up in Orlando, Florida, just 50 miles from Cape Canaveral, and as a college student he helped survey the cape as a possible rocket-launching site. As a highly regarded navy test pilot, Young joined NASA with the second group of astronauts in 1962. During the next ten years he was chosen for four spaceflights—*Gemini 3, Gemini 10, Apollo 10,* and *Apollo 16.* By 1973 Young headed the astronaut office for the new Space Shuttle program, and two years later he was named chief of the astronaut office. Today he continues to direct the training of a new generation of astronauts—men and women—for future spaceflights of their own. More than any other astronaut, John Young has bridged the gap between the old and new eras of space travel.

Columbia *glides toward a landing on the desert runway in California.*

In the distance a silent airplane glided toward a sunbaked runway in California's Mojave Desert. Nearby a quarter-million people looked skyward as the strangely-shaped plane grew larger and larger. The huge crowd was excited because this was no ordinary aircraft. It was an airplane that had just returned from space—a plane that was really the Space Shuttle *Columbia.*

As the *Columbia* touched down smoothly on the desert runway, "The Star Spangled Banner" rang out from hundreds of small radios. Inside the spacecraft the Shuttle commander, John Young, was at the controls. Young had guided *Columbia* to a picture-perfect landing—a landing that made history. For the first time a spacecraft had returned to earth like an airplane.

John Young had made history in another way, too. *Columbia*'s return marked the end of his fifth spaceflight—more than any other astronaut.

Across the country and around the world, people praised America's Space Shuttle. No one could be prouder than John Young's father in Orlando, Florida.

John grew up in Orlando in the heart of Florida's fruit-growing country. Orange, lime, and grapefruit trees covered the gently rolling land for miles and miles. Orlando is about fifty miles from Cape Canaveral on the Atlantic coast. Today there is a large space center there where many spaceships are launched. In the 1930s, however, few people even dreamed that one day spaceflight would be possible.

John's family had moved to Orlando from San Francisco where he was born on September 24, 1930. The Youngs lived there until John was almost two years old.

At that time people were suffering because of the Great Depression. Millions of people could

Rows of citrus trees cover the land near Orlando where John grew up.

not find jobs, and many went hungry. Banks closed. Families lost their homes. Like many others, the Youngs were finding it hard to make ends meet. Finally, John's parents decided to move to Florida. There, they believed, life would be better.

After the outbreak of World War II, John's father, Hugh Young, joined the U.S. Navy. He became a commander in the Seabees. The Seabees built air bases where Navy planes could take off and land. Following the war, Mr. Young became the manager of a fruit farm near Orlando.

John liked to hear his father tell stories about the war. Hugh Young told his son about the German V-2 rocket bombs. During the war the Germans led the world in rocket design. The bombs they put in their V-2 rockets destroyed many buildings and people in Europe.

Before long John wanted to learn all about rockets and flying. Often he drew pictures of different kinds of airplanes and rockets. And he decided that when he grew up, he would like to be a Navy pilot.

At Orlando High School John was a straight "A" student and a member of the honor society. He took part in sports, too. John played guard on the football team, and he was a relay runner in track and field. As a senior he was given the school's highest honor, the Guernsey Good Citizenship Cup.

One of John Young's friends in high school was John Demopoulos. "He [John Young] was always the leader of the class," Demopoulos remembers. "If not the top, then one of the top three. I know he got me through physics."

After high school John went to the Georgia Institute of Technology in Atlanta, called Georgia Tech. He studied aeronautical engineering, which had to do with airplane design. John was happy because he was learning a lot about airplanes and flying.

In his spare time, John liked to dance the jitterbug and listen to music by Spike Jones. Jones was a well-known band leader of the time. John also enjoyed tinkering with gadgets. The more complicated the gadgets, the better he liked them.

One summer during college, John became a member of a survey team. Survey teams measure and map out areas of land. John's team traveled to Cape Canaveral, a lonely, sandy cape just off the east coast of Florida. The team's job was to find out if the cape would be a good rocket-launching site. Little did John know that one day he would be launched into space from that very place.

When John first came to Cape Canaveral, there was no space center there.

In 1952 John graduated from Georgia Tech and joined the U.S. Navy. As soon as his training was completed, he became a Navy pilot. Now John was flying the fastest planes in the sky.

In the Navy John met a young woman he really liked, Barbara Vincent White from Savannah, Georgia. John and Barbara were married in 1955.

Four years later John Young went to Navy test pilot school. Test pilots flew and tested the performance of new aircraft. Young learned how to make sure that new planes were safe and worked properly. He knew that being a test pilot could be dangerous, but he didn't mind.

Hugh Young remembers that he didn't really know what his son was training for at the test pilot school. "I was under the impression that it was a regular school," he says. "I didn't realize that there was anything dangerous about it at all."

The Navy thought so highly of John Young that they sent him to the air station at Point

Mugu, California, for Project High Jump. Project High Jump tested the time-to-climb performance of certain aircraft. That meant the test pilots would try to fly their planes as high as they could in as short a time as possible.

Young flew a F4B Phantom jet. Soaring up into the sky, the Phantom reached a height of 25,000 meters (15½ miles) in less than 4 minutes. John Young had set a new world time-to-climb record.

Young logged many hours in fighter jets like the Phantom, and he loved every moment of flying. "I have the best job in the Navy," he said.

There was one job, however, that Young liked better than any in the Navy. He wanted to be an astronaut, or space pilot, for the National Aeronautics and Space Administration (NASA). NASA was charged with setting up a program to explore outer space. At first NASA launched only unmanned spacecraft, known as satellites. Soon, though, it began a manned spacecraft program called Project Mercury.

John Young had watched the early Mercury flights with keen interest. When he learned that more astronauts were needed, he applied for the job. Hundreds of other pilots applied, too, and NASA picked 253 of the top names. That was still too many, though, because NASA needed just 9 astronauts. On September 17, 1962, NASA announced the names of the 9 men it had chosen. Among them was John Watts Young.

When the news reached the Young home, Barbara jumped for joy. "I just knew you could do it," she told her husband. Barbara told the exciting news to their two children, Sandra and John, Jr.

The Youngs moved to a new house in El Lago, Texas, near NASA's Manned Spacecraft Center in Houston. Most of the astronauts' training would take place at the space center.

The training began almost at once. After three months of classroom study, the astronauts went on long field trips. In jungles and in deserts, the men learned how to survive without food or water. That way they would know what to do if

A NASA instructor shows astronauts how to prepare food in the jungles of Panama. (John Young is standing second from left.)

their spacecraft landed in the wrong place. They found out what it was like to be weightless by flying in a special plane.

Project Mercury had come to an end, and Project Gemini was being planned. The Gemini spacecraft was much larger than the Mercury craft. Gemini capsules would carry two astronauts—a pilot and a co-pilot. They were designed to train astronauts in the skills needed to fly to the moon and back.

Each astronaut worked on part of the Gemini spacecraft or its equipment. John Young's job was to help design safety equipment to protect the men during flight. Some of the Gemini astronauts would leave their capsules on space walks. They would need protection from the extreme heat and cold and blinding light of space. They would also need a strong tether, or cord, to prevent them from floating away from the capsule. Unlike the earth, there is no gravity in space to hold things in place.

Learning to be an astronaut was not easy. Young was surprised by how much he was required to know. "When I came aboard the space program," he said later, "I felt like the greenest rookie in spring training. I had a lot of catching up to do."

By the start of Project Gemini, John Young

John Young during a training session for a space-flight.

was all caught up and ready to go. The pilot of the first manned Gemini flight, Virgil Grissom, chose John Young as his co-pilot. Grissom had this to say about Young. "Sometimes John strikes me as a country boy. The way he walks you would expect him to be holding onto a couple of plow handles instead of a control stick. But he's sharp. And he often gets impatient with the progress we're making. He also has a fine sense of humor. It's a bit unusual and takes you a while to catch onto, but he knows how to ease the strain."

Grissom named the *Gemini 3* spacecraft *Molly Brown* after a musical play, *The Unsinkable Molly Brown*. On Grissom's first Mercury space-flight, his capsule sank after splashdown when the hatch blew off too soon. At the time the capsule was floating upside down in the Atlantic Ocean. Grissom scrambled out and swam in the water with his heavy space suit on until he was rescued. For the *Gemini 3* flight he wanted the capsule to be unsinkable, just like Molly Brown.

On March 23, 1965, *Gemini 3* blasted off a

launch pad at Cape Canaveral. Millions of people watched the launch from the nearby beaches and on TV. As the rocket roared skyward, Young had a fantastic view out of the spacecraft's window. 'There aren't words in the English language to describe the beauty," he said later. "Bermuda glowed like a diamond beneath us. I had work to do, but it took a great effort to get my head back into the cockpit."

The liftoff of Gemini 3. *John Young and Virgil Grissom are riding in* Molly Brown *on top of the spacecraft.*

Molly Brown circled the earth at a height of 120 miles. John Young had many things to do during the flight. One of his jobs was to keep track of the air supply and temperature inside the capsule. Once he noticed that something had gone wrong with the oxygen system. If it wasn't fixed quickly, the astronauts might run out of oxygen to breathe. Young spotted the problem right away and brought the system back to normal. *Molly Brown* continued its mission far above the earth.

Halfway through the flight, Young surprised Grissom by taking out a corned beef sandwich he had smuggled on board. The regular space foods—freeze-dried orange juice, apple sauce, and pot roast—weren't exactly tasty treats. Young had fun with the secret sandwich until NASA found out about it. Before the flight he said, "If you couldn't laugh at yourself sometimes in the space program, I think you'd go right out of your mind."

Sandwiches in space, however, were against the rules because crumbs floating inside the capsule could damage equipment. Later NASA warned the astronauts never to smuggle anything on board a spacecraft again.

In all *Molly Brown* made three orbits of the earth. Five hours after liftoff, it splashed down in the Atlantic Ocean. Young and Grissom bobbed up and down in a choppy sea until a helicopter picked them up. Soon they were safely aboard the U.S. Navy recovery ship, the *Intrepid*.

Later the astronauts visited President Lyndon B. Johnson at the White House. The president gave each of them medals. In New York City they were showered by confetti from tall buildings as they rode by in a tickertape parade. In Chicago a million people lined the streets to see the famous space travelers. John Young was honored by his old school, Georgia Tech, and the navy gave him the rank of commander.

John Young's next spaceflight was *Gemini 10*. On this mission he was the commander, and Michael Collins was his co-pilot. Shortly before *Gemini 10*'s liftoff, an unmanned spacecraft, *Agena 10*, was launched into orbit. Young and

Collins would try to connect, or dock, *Gemini 10* with *Agena 10* in space.

Docking was a very difficult thing to do. Three times astronauts had tried to dock one spacecraft with a second craft, and three times they had failed. Yet docking was an important step in flights to the moon. In fact, it would not be possible to land on the moon without being able to dock two spacecraft.

Gemini 10 was launched from the cape on July 18, 1966. Two hours after launch, Young and Collins caught up with *Agena 10*. As they came nearer, though, Young saw that they were on the wrong course for docking. Taking control of *Gemini 10*, he skillfully docked the two spacecraft.

Agena 10 had a rocket engine of its own that Young could fire from inside *Gemini 10*. At his command the linked Gemini-Agena flew 300 miles higher into space. Its new orbit was 475 miles above the earth, higher than anyone had ever flown before. "That was really something," Young exclaimed into his radio.

Agena 10 *as seen from* Gemini 10 *just before docking. At this point the two spacecraft are just 43 feet apart.*

After three days in space, *Gemini 10* splashed down in the Atlantic on July 21. Young and Collins landed only three miles from the U.S.S. *Guadalcanal.*

In 1966, after two more Gemini flights, the Gemini program ended. Now NASA began the program that would take astronauts to the moon: Project Apollo. The Apollo spaceships were much larger than the Gemini craft and carried a crew of three instead of two. Huge Saturn rockets boosted the Apollo capsules into space.

An Apollo spacecraft was made up of three main parts: a Saturn rocket, a command module, and a lunar module. The rocket would drop away after liftoff. The command module would carry the astronauts from the earth to the moon and back again. And the lunar module would fly from the command module to the moon and back.

NASA planned four manned Apollo flights before the lunar landing. The last of these flights, *Apollo 10,* would do everything *Apollo 11* would do, except land on the moon. *Apollo 10*'s lunar module would make a practice run. It would fly to a point nine miles above the moon, and then return to the command module.

Apollo 10's command module was named *Char-*

The Apollo 10 *command module just before it was joined with its lunar module in the Kennedy Space Center Operations Building at Cape Canaveral.*

lie Brown after the star of the cartoon strip, "Peanuts." John Young would pilot it. The lunar module was named *Snoopy,* just like Charlie Brown's dog. Thomas Stafford and Eugene Cernan would fly it. Young's job was to orbit the moon while Stafford and Cernan flew *Snoopy* close to the surface.

Apollo 10 blasted off the cape on May 18, 1969. After two orbits of the earth, it began the 240,000-mile-long trip to the moon.

Near the halfway point of their trip, the astronauts put on a TV show for earthbound viewers. The TV camera showed the earth from *Apollo 10* and the crew inside the command module. The show started with the crew playing a Frank Sinatra tape of "Fly Me to the Moon." Eugene Cernan held up drawings of Charlie Brown in space coveralls and Snoopy wearing the scarf of the World War I flying ace. John Young may have given Cernan some tips about his drawings. To ease the strain of training, Young drew cartoon sketches of his fellow astronauts.

The earth as it appeared to the Apollo astronauts during their trip to the moon. Near the center of the globe, the United States and Mexico can be seen.

Once during the TV show the camera showed Thomas Stafford and Young side by side. One thing was wrong—Young was upside down. Being in that position didn't seem to bother him, though, because he was weightless. Stafford showed just how weightless Young was by moving him up and down with a touch of his hand. Young joked, "I do everything he tells me."

Three days away from earth, *Charlie Brown* and *Snoopy* slipped into an orbit 69 miles above the moon. Looking out from their spacecraft, the astronauts saw large craters, hills, and mountains. They also saw flat, smooth areas called seas. The "seas" of the moon are dry because there is no water there.

Later John Young described the scene. "The moon was colorful. Not just shades of gray or black and white. It had light tans in it, brilliant whites, and the blackest blacks you ever saw. In the middle of the day the surface was so bright you could hardly stand to look at it.

"Many craters had boulder fields around them.

Craters of all sizes cover much of the far side of the moon.

Some of the boulders must have been 300 feet high. You could see them, with the naked eye, from 60 miles away. We could look down inside the craters and see their walls and floors."

On the far side of the moon, Stafford and Cernan crawled into *Snoopy*. The two ships drew apart, and *Snoopy* flew down toward the moon. Soon it reached its goal—a point just nine miles from the surface. That was closer to the moon than anyone had ever been before.

Commander Stafford was excited by the view. He radioed to earth, "We is down among them, Charlie!" Then he and Cernan scouted the Sea of Tranquillity, where *Apollo 11* was to land. The men reported that it looked very smooth and would make a good landing site.

Meanwhile, John Young continued to orbit the moon in *Charlie Brown*. He heard everything that happened to *Snoopy* on his radio. Young was so busy that he did not have time to grow lonely. Still, he was glad to see Stafford and Cernan return to join him.

Snoopy *returns to join* Charlie Brown *in orbit around the moon.*

After more than two days circling the moon, *Apollo 10* began the journey home. *Charlie Brown* splashed down in the Pacific Ocean near the island of Pago Pago. There the astronauts were greeted by five thousand people waving American flags.

Back in the United States, Young, Stafford, and Cernan were treated as national heroes.

(From left to right) Thomas Stafford, John Young, and Eugene Cernan at a postflight news conference. Snoopy (lower right) came along, too.

John Young had been through all the parades and speeches before. He was an old pro at space travel now, but he couldn't wait to start training for another flight. For him being an astronaut was the best job in the world. "I can't think of another single job I'd rather have," he said.

Two months after the flight of *Apollo 10,* astronauts Neil Armstrong and Buzz Aldrin made the first moon landing. But that wasn't the end of Project Apollo. NASA planned for six more Apollo flights. Now that the moon had been reached, it must be explored.

John Young was named to command *Apollo 16.* His crewmates were Charles Duke, Jr., and Thomas Mattingly. On this flight Young and Duke would land on the moon in the lunar module *Orion.* Mattingly would fly the command module *Casper.*

Apollo 16's mission was to explore the lunar highlands. The highlands was one of the most rugged parts of the moon. It had never been explored, and the landing would be very risky.

Apollo 16 lifted off from Cape Canaveral on April 16, 1972. After the long trip to the moon, *Orion* and *Casper* undocked. Just as they began to move apart, one of *Casper*'s control systems failed.

If the control system didn't work, the astronauts might be left in space, unable to return. Back on earth, NASA scientists quickly studied the problem. For four hours *Orion* and *Casper* stayed just a few feet apart. At last mission control radioed that the problem was solved. All systems were "go" for *Orion* to land on the moon.

Orion landed safely in the Cayley Plains, a flat region high in the Descartes Mountains. John Young was the first to climb down *Orion*'s ladder, and the ninth person ever to step onto the moon. Soon Charles Duke joined him.

Young and Duke went to work. They set up instruments for use in scientific tests, placed TV cameras for viewers on earth, and raised an American flag. Finally they unloaded the lunar Rover from *Orion*'s cargo hold.

John Young jumps up off the moon as he salutes the American flag.

The Rover was a four-wheeled, electric-powered moon car. Riding in the Rover, the astronauts could explore many miles from their landing site. They took their moon car for a spin as soon as it was all put together.

The next day Young and Duke drove the Rover

Astronaut Young reaches for some tools in the back of his moon car, the Rover.

partway up Stone Mountain. There the astronauts enjoyed a bird's-eye view of the plains below. They could see *Orion* not far from several craters—Ravine, Wreck, Stubby, and North Ray. "What a sight," Charlie Duke exclaimed. "You can't believe the view. It's super."

On the third day the men made their most daring trip in the Rover. They drove to the edge of North Ray Crater, three miles from *Orion*. North Ray was nearly a mile across and more than six hundred feet deep. Young and Duke threaded their way down the steep slopes of the crater. Inside, North Ray was filled with huge boulders. The men chipped samples from the boulders and gathered soil and rocks.

John Young (far left) looks at a big boulder on the moon.

In all Young and Duke spent 71 hours on the moon, longer than any Apollo crew before them. The astronauts brought back 214 pounds of lunar rocks and soil and many moon photos. On earth scientists would study the rocks, soil, and pictures to learn how the moon was formed.

When *Orion* returned to *Casper, Apollo 16* headed back to earth. It splashed down in the Pacific Ocean just a mile off the bow of the U.S.S. *Ticonderoga.* The mission had been a big success. In John Young's words, "We saw as much in ten days as most people see in ten lifetimes."

For ten years Young had worked long and hard for NASA. Much of the time he had to be away from his family while training for a spaceflight. Before his *Gemini 3* mission, Young described the life of an astronaut. "Right now I'm eating, breathing, and sleeping this flight."

Barbara Young wanted John to spend more time with her and the two children. John did not want to give up his career as an astronaut. Finally, in 1972, he and Barbara were divorced.

The old pro of the astronauts in the cockpit of an air force jet.

Later John married Susy Feldman of Saint Louis, Missouri.

After Project Apollo John Young was the old pro among the NASA astronauts. In 1973 NASA chose him to head the astronaut office for their new spacecraft program, the Space Shuttle. Two years later he was named chief of the astronaut office. As chief he was in charge of all the astronauts in the space program. Young made sure that each astronaut received the proper training for spaceflight. And he gave each one a job to help the designers and engineers of the Space Shuttle.

The Shuttle is unlike any spacecraft that flew before it. In fact, it is so different that many people thought it would not work. The key part of the Shuttle, called the orbiter, is a cargo plane for space. That means it can carry things like satellites from the earth into space. Satellites orbit the earth in places that make it possible for them to do special jobs. Communications satellites beam TV and radio signals all over the world. Spy satellites take pictures of military bases.

The Space Shuttle orbiter has wings and a rudder and looks like a stubby airplane. At launch it is bolted to three rockets. Two of these are thin, solid fuel rocket boosters. These powerful boosters had never been used to launch astronauts before. The third is a large, liquid fuel rocket like the ones used for Apollo flights.

Just like earlier craft, the Shuttle takes off from a launch pad. Before it leaves the earth's atmosphere, the rockets drop away. In space the Shuttle orbiter flies like an airplane, only upside down. When it is time to come back to earth, the orbiter becomes an airplanelike glider. Like an airplane, it lands on a runway.

Earlier spaceships could be flown into space just once. The Shuttle orbiter, however, can be flown into space again and again. In fact, NASA says that each orbiter can make one

The Space Shuttle on its way to the launch pad.

hundred flights or more. Because it can be reused, the Shuttle costs less money to fly than other spaceships. That means more flights into space can be made than ever before. And on each flight an orbiter can carry several satellites into space. Earlier spacecraft could carry just one. Imagine the number of satellites that one orbiter could carry in a hundred spaceflights!

During the 1970s NASA chose the orbiter *Columbia* to make the first Shuttle flight into space. John Young was named as the Space Shuttle commander. His co-pilot was Robert Crippen, a rookie astronaut.

Young and Crippen would fly *Columbia* into space and back to earth. On this first test flight, they would carry no satellites with them. Their only job was to make sure that the Shuttle flew and its systems worked. They would be its test pilots.

The astronauts began a tough training schedule. They did classroom work and studied the Shuttle's 21-volume flight manual. Young and

John Young (far right) jogging with Robert Crippen (center) and Vice-President George Bush (far left).

Crippen spent many hours practicing flight plans in an exact model of *Columbia*'s cockpit. To get a better feel for *Columbia* as an airplane, they flew Boeing 707 jets.

Before the Shuttle could be launched into space, many design problems had to be solved. First the rocket engines wouldn't work. Then the heat tiles kept falling off the orbiter. *Columbia* would become red-hot when it returned to earth from space. The heat tiles kept the spacecraft from burning up as it came back into the earth's atmosphere. At last, after many delays, the problems were solved. *Columbia* was ready, and John Young and Robert Crippen were waiting for the "go" for launch.

At dawn on April 12, 1981, more than a million people watched *Columbia* from beaches near the Cape Canaveral launch site. Millions more watched and listened on TV and radio. Reporters had come from around the world to cover the first flight of the Space Shuttle. Would this daring new spacecraft work? they wondered. John Young and Robert Crippen believed it would work. They were betting their lives on it.

Suddenly *Columbia*'s three main engines roared to life. The thundering blast shook the earth for miles around. Then the two powerful solid fuel rockets lit up the sky like Roman candles. As *Columbia* soared skyward, people in the crowd shouted, "Go, man, go." "Fly like an eagle." "Smooth sailing, baby."

The Space Shuttle blasts off from the cape. On the left of the spacecraft, the orbiter Columbia rides gracefully on its first journey into space.

Strapped into the pilot's seat, John Young looked straight up into the blue Florida sky. After four spaceflights, this liftoff didn't cause him to lose his cool. Robert Crippen, the rookie astronaut, was more excited. "Man, what a feeling! What a view!" he exclaimed. "Glad you're enjoying it," replied Mission Control in Houston.

In just eight minutes *Columbia* was far out over the Atlantic Ocean. Soon the three rockets fell away, and the spacecraft went into orbit 150 miles above the earth. Traveling at 17,500 miles per hour, it sped around the world once every 90 minutes.

At the start of the second orbit, the crew opened the big doors to the cargo bay. Although nothing was in the bay now, the doors had to be opened to cool off the inside of the ship. Otherwise, the heat from the equipment inside would grow too great. On later Shuttle flights the cargo bay will hold satellites. A long metal arm will lift the satellites out and release them into space.

TV cameras on *Columbia* showed the cargo

Columbia's cargo bay with its door open in space.

bay doors open and close. The cameras also showed something that surprised Mission Control. A handful of the more than thirty thousand heat tiles had fallen off the spacecraft on both sides of the tail section. If too many tiles came loose, *Columbia* would burn up when it returned to earth. Soon Mission Control announced that the missing tiles were not that important. The tiles were on the side of the craft that would not get red-hot during reentry.

Young and Crippen spent two days in space. They tested all of *Columbia*'s systems, and everything worked. Although the astronauts were busy, they did take time out to sleep. Mission Control woke them up by playing a loud song about the Shuttle called "The Mean Machine."

Commander Young reported that his ship "is performing just outstanding." *Columbia* was much easier to fly than other spaceships Young had piloted. In fact, most of the real work on the Shuttle was done by computers. The astronauts' main job was to make sure the computers were doing the right thing at the right time.

Young and Crippen did have a few things to complain about. Once, without warning, the cabin temperature dropped to a chilly 37 degrees. "I was ready to break out the long undies," joked Young. A signal from Mission Control soon warmed up the cold astronauts.

On April 14 *Columbia* began the return to earth over the Pacific Ocean. Within minutes the heat tiles on the belly and wings of the ship were

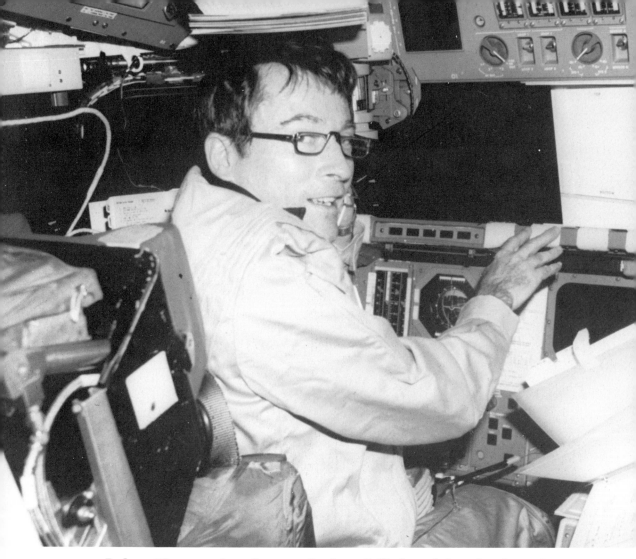

John Young in the cockpit of Columbia *during its first, history-making flight.*

flaming hot. Hot gases around the spacecraft caused a 21-minute loss of radio contact with earth. Just before the blackout, Mission Control radioed, "Nice and easy does it, John. We are all riding with you."

All the heat tiles stayed on, and *Columbia* safely reentered the earth's atmosphere. Now John Young took control from the spacecraft's computers. Young made a series of sharp S-loops over the Pacific to cut down *Columbia*'s great speed. Still, the ship was flying at 5,000 miles per hour as it flew over the west coast of the United States. "What a way to come to California," exclaimed Crippen.

Before landing Young made one final loop. Then he began to guide *Columbia* down toward the desert runway at Edwards Air Force Base in California. The runway was a dry lakebed, as hard and smooth as concrete. Nearby the huge crowd waited for the first sight of the spacecraft.

Columbia dropped noiselessly through the desert sky. It was a gliding airplane now. There were no computers or engines to set its course—only John Young. Young pulled the ship's nose up sharply, lowered the landing gear, and touched down gently at a speed of 215 miles per hour. A cloud of dust rose from *Columbia*'s wheels. Slowly the

With John Young at the controls, Columbia *touches down on a desert runway in California.*

large craft rolled to a stop while the crowd roared its approval. "Welcome home, *Columbia*. Beautiful. Beautiful," said Mission Control.

All over America people gathered to watch the end of *Columbia*'s history-making flight. Teachers stopped their classes so that students could see the landing. Work came to a halt in many offices and factories. At Georgia Tech, Young's old school, a band played "I'm a ramblin' wreck from Georgia Tech." *Columbia*'s flight seemed to give the whole country a lift. President Reagan expressed the joy of the nation when he praised astronauts Young and Crippen. "Through you we feel as giants once again," said the president.

John Young was excited by *Columbia*'s landing, too. When Mission Control told him that he could get out of the spacecraft, he ran down the stairs. On the ground he checked out the heat tiles and the landing gear. That was just what a good test pilot should do after a flight. Then Young smiled, jumped up and jabbed the air with his fist. The old pro had finally lost his cool.

Columbia's flight marked the beginning of a new era in space. The Shuttle is the key part of NASA's planned Space Transportation System (STS). When STS is complete, *Columbia* will be joined by at least three other orbiters—*Challenger, Discovery,* and *Atlantis.* Each of these orbiters can make at least one hundred spaceflights and carry hundreds of satellites. In that way STS will make each spaceflight cost less and do more than earlier flights. By 1985 Shuttle flights may be taking off every few weeks.

The Shuttle also brightens the future for space science. On the second Shuttle flight, radar signals were beamed toward the earth. These signals made a maplike picture that may help scientists find new sources of energy on earth. Other tests on the flight measured air and water pollution in different parts of the earth.

In 1985 a large telescope will be placed in orbit during a shuttle flight. High above the earth's atmosphere, the telescope will be able to see much farther than it could on earth. Scientists hope that this telescope will show them how big the universe is.

The U.S. Air Force is interested in the Shuttle, too. At least 21 of the first 68 planned Shuttle flights will carry military cargo such as Big Bird spy satellites. Some people are afraid that the Shuttle will start an arms race in space. Others say that it will be used more for peaceful projects.

At the time of *Columbia*'s flight, John Young was 50 years old. He had flown five space missions—more missions than any other astronaut. Inside NASA new astronauts—men and women—were being trained for future spaceflights. Almost all the old trailblazing astronauts were gone. Some had retired, while others had gone into business and politics. The pioneering days of spaceflight were over.

John Young has bridged the gap between the old and the new eras. After nearly twenty years as an astronaut, he is still going strong. Young continues his job at NASA as chief of the astronaut office. He wants to make sure that those new astronauts have the very best of training before they lift off on a spaceflight of their own.

How long will Young keep on soaring into space? "The rest of his life," says his old friend, John Demopoulos. "As long as they need him. He's invaluable to the program."

John Young hasn't made plans for another spaceflight, but *Columbia*'s flight is one that he will long remember. After his return to earth, Young explained why the flight was so special to him. "We're not really too far—the human race isn't too far from going to the stars. Bob and I are mighty proud to have been a part of that evolution."

The photographs are reproduced through the courtesy of the National Aeronautics and Space Administration and the Florida Department of Commerce, Division of Tourism.

The Author

Paul Westman is a regular contributor to *Current Biography* and has written many books for young people, including several for the Taking Part series. Of the series, Westman says, "Young readers will learn something about well-known contemporary men and women in many challenging fields and at the same time begin to discover some of the joys of reading."

A recent graduate of the University of Minnesota, Westman lives in Minneapolis.